EMOTIONAL AVENUES

Feeling How We Work

TOM DESPARD

*Author of **Performance Avenue**s and **T**ouch*

Copyright © 2016 by Tom Despard

Emotional Avenues
Feeling How We Work
by Tom Despard

Printed in the United States of America.

ISBN 9781498462396

All rights reserved solely by the author. The author guarantees all contents are original and do not infringe upon the legal rights of any other person or work. No part of this book may be reproduced in any form without the permission of the author. The views expressed in this book are not necessarily those of the publisher.

Unless otherwise indicated, Scripture quotations taken from the Holy Bible, New International Version (NIV). Copyright © 1973, 1978, 1984, 2011 by Biblica, Inc.™. Used by permission. All rights reserved.

www.xulonpress.com

Other books by Tom Despard

Performance Avenues
The Top Line
Winter Wind
Turning the Stones
Finding Your Clown
Red Barns and Green Fields
Touch

Table of Contents

You Can Just Feel It vii

Table of Emotional Avenues at Work xiii

The Emotional Avenues of the Leader. 17

The Emotional Avenues of the Learner. 27

The Emotional Avenues of the Innovator. 37

The Emotional Avenues of the Manager. 47

The Emotional Avenues of the Promoter 55

Some Final Feelings. 63

Journal of Catching Yourself Feeling at Work. 69

You Can Just Feel It

Emotional Avenues, Feeling How We Work, was inspired by my research and development for *Performance Avenues, Knowing How We Work* and for *Touch, Waking Up to the Power of Positive Emotions* and is a synthesis of both. How and why we perform at work is critical to our success. The hot topics of emotional intelligence and decision-making with our feelings need simple intuitive tools for application in the workplace and in the rest of our lives. These two previous books, each about a two-hour read, are prerequisites for this book as is a review of our website at www.PerformanceAvenues.com.

Emotional Avenues is an outgrowth of *Performance Avenues* where we have developed the groundbreaking concept of Performance Types that we recommend be used along with Personality Types in the assessment of who we are and how we most naturally, comfortably and effectively perform on the job. *Emotional Avenues* is a self-help business book, but it's not another one on emotional intelligence (as broad and helpful as these books are) that explains, for example, how to overcome codependency or respond to fear. It is rather an important component of understanding the assessment of skills needed for a Leader, a Learner, an Innovator, Manager and a Promoter.

We are again breaking new ground in the way we have included emotional characteristics and their adaptability and application by people as these characteristics relate to their Performance Types. And again the emphasis here is one of simplicity and intuitiveness so that the awareness about feelings derived from Emotional Avenues can be easily put to good use right away and perfected with practice over time.

Our "avenues" approach has the practical advantage of being effectively used for individuals, teams, companies, and organizations especially since the same definitions, principles, format and questions can be applied to all of them. So, for example, an individual, a team, a company or an organization can all lead with courage, learn with curiosity, and promote with engagement.

My research for *Touch* confirmed that Emotional Avenues needed to be part of Performance Avenues to provide for more comprehensive assessments. It's been a matter of applying what is known about emotional intelligence to individuals, teams and companies within the Performance Avenues framework. Emotional Avenues is now part of our self-assessment process as well as our *Directions Workshop* which is available for your group, team, company or organization — see our website at www.PerformanceAvenues.com for details.

Assessments and descriptions of work traits and types have traditionally centered much more on thinking than feeling. And yet feeling drives our reasoning and behavior more or less as much as thinking and more so in quick decision-making. French mathematician and philosopher Blaise Pascal (he is well worth googling) had this to offer regarding the heart, emotions and reasoning:

> The heart has its reasons which reason knows nothing of.

> We know truth, not only by reason, but also by the heart.

Clarity of mind means clarity of passion, too; this is why a great and clear mind loves ardently and sees distinctly what it loves.

So we have to think and feel about our emotions in order to get the right handle on our reasoning and behavior at work and in the rest of our lives. *We can't just think though a problem, we have to feel through it as well.* For example, the Manager, above all else, needs to be in touch with reality — and his or her level of "authenticity." The Innovator needs to understand his or her level of measured risk-taking and their "daring" quotient.

The subtitle of this book is *Feeling How We Work*. Feeling is generally described as the response to an emotion — but as with most books on emotions and feelings, we are going to use these two terms more or less interchangeably. We have to feel our feelings. For example, at any given time, to what degree are we passionate, patient, vulnerable, committed or encouraging? How aware are we of how our emotions are affecting our decisions and behavior? As with *Touch*, this book deals only with positive emotions — not that the negative ones are not important and need to be addressed, but let's see how we can crowd them out with positive thinking and feeling. There's plenty of helpful information on topics such as anger management and shame resilience that I will leave to qualified others to provide.

The following findings of Megan Biro fits well with this concept in that reaching people on an emotional level is more effective than reaching them on a rational level — though both are critical. She is describing the Leader here, but whatever Performance Avenue we are predominantly on, enhancing our emotional outreach has a huge effect on how others perceive us and how well we relate to them.

Megan M. Biro, Contributor to Forbes Magazine:
(http://www.forbes.com/sites/
meghanbiro/2013/12/15/
leadership-is-about-emotion/)

Make a list of the 5 leaders you most admire. They can be from business, social media, politics, technology, the sciences, any field. Now ask yourself why you admire them. The chances are high that your admiration is based on more than their accomplishments, impressive as those may be. I'll bet that everyone on your list reaches you on an *emotional* level.

This ability to reach people in a way that transcends the intellectual and rational is the mark of a great leader. They all have it. They inspire us. It's a simple as that. And when we're inspired we tap into our best selves and deliver amazing work.

So, can this ability to touch and inspire people be learned? No and yes. The truth is that not everyone can lead, and there is no substitute for natural talent. Honestly, I'm more convinced of this now — I'm in reality about the world of work and employee engagement. But for those who fall somewhat short of being a natural born star (which is pretty much many of us), leadership skills can be acquired, honed and perfected. And when this happens, your chances of engaging your talent increases from the time they walk into your culture.

We can enhance this emotional outreach by aligning Emotional Avenues with Performance Avenues and thereby identifying certain emotions and their role in determining how we go about our work. As you can see from the *Table on Emotional Avenues at Work* which follows this section, each Performance Avenue of Leader,

Learner, Innovator, Manager and Promoter has a primary driving emotion and four other key emotions associated with it. These Emotional Avenues provide for a more well-rounded conversation about how we perform on each Performance Avenue. For example, do you as a Leader have humility? Are you as a Manager committed to the mission? Do you as a Learner seek wisdom?

We have attached five of the most significant and compelling positive Emotional Avenues for each Performance Avenue. The one listed first for each avenue such as "Appeal" for Promoter is the most important one for that avenue. This exercise is an art and a science gleaned from many years of experience in the workplace and on non-profit boards, consulting engagements, my two books mentioned above, and a broad review of the published research on emotions at work. It's enlightening and often critical for us to be more aware of the emotions we have and need and the emotions our coworkers have and need.

Emotional Avenues is a tool for expressing emotions as they relate to how someone performs at work. David Rock in *Your Brain at Work* points out that "... a lot of people, especially in the business world, don't discuss their feelings." That reinforces why we added emotions to Performance Avenues — to be more actively expressive about emotions and more deeply engaged in understanding who we are and how we work.

A final note before we begin. There are about 800,000 personality and performance assessments and some, such as the *BestWork DATA* assessments created by Chuck Russell, can be quite helpful if chosen and applied appropriately. Since we are the ones who know the most about who we really are, any personality and performance assessments need to be combined with a self-assessment of ourselves. As Isabel Briggs Myers asserts, *"It is up to each person to recognize his or her true preferences."* Use this book as one tool in your self-awareness toolbox.

Thank you and happy reading.

Let me know you feel about *Emotional Avenues* at:

tdespard@PerfomanceAvenues.com

Table of Emotional Avenues at Work

LEADER
Courage
Trust
Inspiration
Passion
Humility

LEARNER
Curiosity
Patience
Wisdom
Faith
Fairness

INNOVATOR
Daring
Perseverance
Vulnerability
Independence
Optimism

MANAGER
Authenticity
Pride
Commitment
Sensing
Empathy

PROMOTER
Appeal
Engagement
Encouragement
Appreciation
Amusement

Emotional Avenues of the Leader

Emotional Avenues of the Leader

More has been written about leaders and leadership in books and articles than any other business workplace subject. Since you are already familiar with a ton of stuff about it, I'm going to sum it up in one quotation by John Quincy Adams:

> If your actions inspire others to dream more, learn more, do more, and become more, you are a leader.

In targeting the Emotional Avenues of the Leader, we begin with Harvey Deutschendorf, author of *The Other Kind of Smart, Simple Ways to Boost Your Emotional Intelligence for Greater Personal Effectiveness and Success*, who has determined that the five ways to spot an emotionally intelligent leader are that he or she is:

1. Non-defensive and open.
2. Aware of their own emotions.
3. Adept at picking up on the emotional state of others.
4. Available for those reporting to them.
5. Able to check their ego and allow others to shine.

Leaders are watched, especially for any signs of their emotions. They influence people and outcomes with their emotions and set the mood of an organization with their mood. If they are upbeat and forward looking, so is their organization's culture. David Rock in *Your Brain at Work* provides this neurological insight:

> The boss's emotions can have a flow-on effect on others, since people pay close attention to the boss. You see the boss smile, and your brain starts to mimic the smile; then you smile; then the boss smiles back. It's a virtuous and upward cycle, with each person raising the depth of the other's smile through a mirroring function. Mirror neurons explain why leaders need to be extra conscious of managing their stress levels, as their emotions really do impact others.

Let's now have a conversation about the key emotions of the Leader's courage, trust, inspiration, passion and humility.

Courage

First let's look at one critical thing that courage is not. In 1519 Ferdinand Magellan, a Portuguese captain sailing for the king of Spain, courageously departed Seville with five ships and 270 men and headed west in search of a sea route to the Spice Islands. He shrewdly put down a mutiny that was followed by a shipwreck, survived the unauthorized escape and return to Spain of another ship, and then swiftly crossed the Pacific with three ships ending up in what is now the Philippines. But there his courage was trumped by pride and bravado that led to his demise. He had made friends with one tribe and in a needless show of force, attacked one of the tribe's enemy tribes and was killed in a foolhardy beach landing by an overwhelming surge of fierce warriors. His expedition finally returned to Spain, with one ship loaded with spices and 18 men. History is replete with such examples. True leaders are courageous but also humble and thoughtful.

The following is from a PowerPoint slide from our *Directions Workshop* which is available by contacting us through our website at: www.PerformanceAvenues.com.

>>> Leading with *Courage*

People, teams and companies need to lead with courage, which Aristotle called the first virtue, because it makes all of the other virtues possible. *Courage* is derived from *cor*, the Latin word for heart. It's the strength of the heart that underlies the confidence, resolve, boldness and bravery to lead effectively. It's the courage of our convictions that overcomes fear and danger and motivates us to take the road less traveled by while inspiring others to take it too.

Do I, our teams, and our company lead with courage?

Courage is so important that it's one of the seven cardinal virtues by way of the concept of "fortitude" from the Latin "fortes" which means strong and powerful. You have often heard the phrase "intestinal fortitude" which connotes resoluteness, endurance and guts. A further discussion of fortitude and the other cardinal virtues is available in my book, *The Top Line, Virtuous Companies Finish First*.

So the Leader faces up to, sorts through, and evaluates fears and dangers and gains confidence by facing and overcoming them. He or she knows their own strengths and weaknesses. The Leader is not afraid to fail knowing that failure is part being successful.

General John Pershing inspected the 1st Division in France in 1917 and harshly critiqued the division and its commander for its many perceived failings. To his surprise, a young captain named George Marshall stepped forward not only to defend his commander, but to also hold Pershing's headquarters responsible for some of the division's problems. Rather than demote or reassign

Marshall for insubordination, Pershing eventually took a liking to Marshall, made him his top aide, and promoted his military career. Marshall's fortitude and fearlessness led him to become Chief of Staff of the Army in 1939 and build the United States war machine from 200,000 troops to more than eight million. He was also the leader for the Marshall Plan that rebuilt Europe after World War II.

Trust

Do you trust your boss? Does he or she trust you? There are no great leaders or great followers without trust. Here's an excellent insight into how critical trust is to leadership today:

> Charles Green, Contributor to Forbes Magazine: http://www.forbes.com/sites/trustedadvisor/2012/04/03/why-trust-is-the-new-core-of-leadership/

> Leaders can no longer trust in power; instead, they rely on the power of trust. Today's leaders are those who can successfully persuade others to trust them will evidence certain behaviors:

> - They themselves will be skilled at trusting, because trusting and trustworthiness enhance each other.
> - They will be good at collaboration and the tools of influence.
> - They will operate from a clear set of values and principles, because opportunistic or selfish motives are clearly seen and rejected.
> - They are likely to be more intrinsically than extrinsically motivated, and more likely to use intrinsic motivations with others.
> - They will not be dependent on direct authority or political power.

In short, leaders in the new business world will be skilled at the art and science of trust.

Verification is simply a matter of the past experience of the Leader. What is his or her track record? Have they been forthcoming, straightforward and honest? But ongoing checking doesn't hurt — sometimes people tell you something that they sincerely believe to be true, but that is either not true or only part of the story. Trust is a treasure that is built up over time, but can be stolen in one incident. A Leader needs to trust and be trusted.

Inspiration

Think of the leaders who have inspired you at work. How did they do it? An in-depth research project is described below — see how you relate to these findings.

> Jack Zenger and Joseph Folkman, Harvard Business Review
> http://blogs.hbr.org/2013/06/
> what-inspiring-leaders-do/
>
> To address this question of what inspiring leaders do and how they do it, we engaged in what some might refer to as a reverse-engineering exercise. We went into our database and looked for those leaders who received the highest scores on the competency of "inspires and motivates to high performance." We found 1,000 such leaders and then analyzed what they did that separated them from their less-inspiring counterparts.
>
> Some of what they did was specific and tangible. For example, they set stretch goals with their team. They spent time developing their subordinates. They engaged in highly collaborative behavior. They encouraged those about them to be more innovative.

Other things we identified were somewhat less specific and less tangible. These inspirational leaders were more adept at making emotional connections with their subordinates, for instance. They were better at establishing a clear vision. They were more effective in their communication and willing to spend more time communicating. They were ardent champions of change. They were perceived as effective role models within the organization.

Inspiration involves a whole set of behaviors and the degree to which those behaviors are acted out. It's a lot more EI that IQ! We are also social beings and inspire others by being friendly and empathetic. Inspiration can simply by measured by the desire and degree to which followers follow the Leader.

Passion

Passion is high on all Leader behavioral trait lists and is a critical and very contagious emotion for everybody in the workplace. I'm extremely passionate about that! But let's take a close look at passion without being blinded by our passion for it.

We need to love most of what we do and like the rest. And we need to be driven by and towards the vision and the mission. The Leader therefore leads with open and well expressed passion like nothing else.

Business thinker and author Ericka Anderson offers this breakdown of leadership passion with these five indicators of a leader who has true passion:

- Commit honestly — Passionate leaders genuinely believe in what they espouse. People are touched and engaged by the genuineness of their passion.

- Make a clear case without being dogmatic — They convey the power of their belief without dismissing or belittling others' points of view.
- Invite real dialogue about their passion — Their passion is balanced with openness: they want to hear and integrate others' points of view.
- Act in support of their passion — They walk their talk: their day-to-day behaviors support their beliefs.
- Stay committed despite adversity and setbacks — Their commitment isn't flimsy; when difficulties arise, they hold to their principles and find a way forward.

When a leader is passionate, she adds, people feel a deep sense of being led in a worthy direction by someone who is committed to something more important than his or her own individual glory.

If you don't have a passion about your work, try to find out why including by expressing your feelings to others. What is there to like or dislike about your work? What can be changed to improve your attitude? This is crucial for the Leader since passion cannot be faked for long.

Humility

Are you humble? Are you proud of your humility? The fifth key emotion for the Leader is humility and without a doubt is the most challenging. The simple fact is that we think we know more than we know. And we seek status, independence and control. We have a lack of self-awareness about our own pride. The Bible is replete with admonitions against pride and encouragements for humility. Proverbs 11:2, "When pride comes, then comes shame, but with the humble comes wisdom." Psalm 147:6a, "The Lord lifts up the humble..." We are not to focus on ourselves, but on others. We are not naturally humble. Therefore we have to *pursue* humility with all we've got.

It's not about giving up on self-confidence, but about having it in abundance. The confident Leader knows he or she is human and needs to be perceived that way. One of Dale Carnegie's most vital axioms is to admit a mistake "quickly and emphatically." The Leader who confesses, "I made a mistake, let's correct it, learn from it, and move on" is one who understands this concept and is respected by his or her teammates. Notice I said "teammates" — treat your associates like they are part of your team and decision-making is improved and productivity goes up.

Listening sincerely and carefully and continually building a consensus are high-marks of humility. A Leader who imposes his own ideas and operates from a top-down position, will not inspire his or her troops. Acknowledgement, collaboration, synergy and transparency are approaches to leading that the Leader can use effectively all day long. Developing people and meeting their needs are also much appreciated acts of humility. The more a Leader is a servant, the more he or she is a true Leader.

You can just feel it

When Leaders are in touch with their emotions of courage, trust, inspiration, passion, humility and other relevant and actionable emotions, they are better Leaders. Do you as a Leader: have the courage of your convictions, have the trust of your associates, inspire others, have expressed passion for your work, and have a true sense of humility? Can you really feel it?

Emotional Avenues of the Learner

Emotional Avenues of the Learner

The Emotional Avenues of the Learner (and the Learner in us) are curiosity, patience, wisdom, faith and fairness. As a Learner-Innovator, I have a heightened sensitivity to these emotions. The Learner is especially attuned at going from data to information to knowledge to understanding and then to wisdom. But that takes curiosity and patience. Faith and fairness flow from wisdom.

We think of learning as strictly rational and logical. But remember feeling drives and directs us our decision-making and behavior as much or more than thinking. Focusing on the emotions of the Learner lights them up and can intensify and improve our motivation and ability to learn. *This is the what, why and how of the Emotional Avenues approach — as we think and feel about critical emotions at work, we measure and deploy them more consciously, intently and usefully.*

There is a significant emotional return on our investment in learning and the many ways we learn. We love to learn. Learning makes us feel better. It sharpens our brains and makes us more aware and confident. We begin with curiosity, which when combined with patience, leads to wisdom and wisdom leads to faith and fairness.

Curiosity

Curiosity is indeed a curious emotion. It's the primary motivation to learn and the foundation of all learning. I like the Wikipedia quote on it:

> **Curiosity** (from Latin *curiosus* "careful, diligent, curious," akin to *cura* "care") is a quality related to inquisitive thinking such as exploration, investigation, and learning, evident by observation in human and many animal species. The term can also be used to denote the behavior itself being caused by the emotion of curiosity. As this emotion represents a thirst for knowledge, curiosity is a major driving force behind scientific research and other disciplines of human study.

We are all naturally curious, but it's a matter of degree — some of us turn over every stone, others are satisfied not to do so as much. And complacency can set in. We may think and feel that we know enough for now and are just trying to get through the events and operations of each day at work. Also, the level of a company's learning culture affects our level of curiosity at work over time.

The solution is a healthy inquisitiveness that asks, for example, why a decision came down as it did. What more do I need to know about my company and about my job in order to exceed expectations, both my own and those of my boss and team members. Put up a "CURIOUS?" sign in your office or perhaps a rough sketch of your current learning curve. Complete some selected personal assessment questionnaires so that you will "know thyself" better.

Intentional conversations are also important to sustaining our curiosity. The more appropriate and timely questions we can pose during a conversation, the more we keep curiosity in our minds. Find out more, get to the "WHY" of things, and peel lots of onions. So when you ask someone to do something as a boss or team leader, explain to them why they will be better off by following your directives or accomplishing a particular the task.

Patience

Patience is an emotion of the Learner because in its active state — and we have to focus on being patient — it provides for more listening, openness, acceptance, clarity and awareness of our mind, body and spirit. It involves self-control, breathing more deeply, getting in touch with what is really happening, and pondering before responding — waiting to be more informed and aware before forming an opinion or acting out. So as we learn to be more patient, we are better prepared to learn more. The answer we are looking for may take time and hard work. And impatience is always there tempting us to take a shortcut.

Being impulsive and jumping to conclusions, which I'm pretty good at, shuts down the learning process and makes us more prone to mistakes. The same thing happens when a fixed mindset prevents us from doing our due diligence in an atmosphere of intentional patience.

While we live in the Information Age, in the United States of America we also live in a "culture of immediacy." We want things, including information, yesterday. We want to run before we have learned to walk. We believe that because we have so much information at our fingertips that we are great scholars. But being a scholar, even a good thinker and feeler, takes deliberate and consistent patience.

I'm amazed at how patience can foster listening and learning. In your workplace, do you think AND feel before you speak? Do you wait for the right answer to surface? Are you patient with people's learning and performance curves? Do you persevere with patience?

Wisdom

I classify wisdom as an emotion because the more emotional maturity we have the wiser we are. Wisdom is more than being intelligent. It is shaped further by experience and enlightenment and the development of our emotional intelligence. A wise person has learned how to become aware of their emotions and work with them in a seasoned and positive way. We can also have those "aha" moments by reflecting, both consciously and subconsciously, on information, understandings and insights that we already have stored in our brains. And pursuant to the theory in my book *Touch*, people need to combine positive emotions such as *wisdom* with "knowmotions" such as *smart* (wisdom's corresponding knowmotion) in order to get "comotions," — that is, a synthesis of what we feel and what we think.

The Book of Proverbs is part of a tradition of wisdom literature and exhorts that fear (awe, respect) is the beginning of all wisdom, that wisdom is more precious that gold or silver, and that wisdom will protect us.

Prudence, another of the seven cardinal virtues described in my book *The Top Line*, is what might be called in modern parlance "advanced wisdom" as might be accessed by clicking onto the "advanced" tab of a computer window. It is, among other things, the exercise of sound judgment which circles back to the need for the emotional maturity mentioned above.

Eighteenth century Puritan Richard Steele emphasizes in *The Religious Tradesman*:

> The first thing necessary for a happy progress in business is prudence and discretion. This, as it relates to trade, is a habit of mind enabling us to conduct our affairs in the

wisest and best manner; or, in other words, it is pursuing the proper end, by the best means, and in the fittest times.

So the Learner develops a prudent "habit of mind" with regard to his or her intellect, emotions, subconscious, and conscience (moral compass) as well as the ability to articulate this reservoir of wisdom to individuals, teams and organizational cultures.

Faith

Curiosity with patience fosters our wisdom, which in turn fosters our faith — a faith that is well grounded and enables us to make the best choices and decisions and display our best behavior. Faith is an emotion of the Learner in us and the more we learn, the more realistic and effective our faith becomes. We are all lifetime Learners and we are all lifetime believers with beliefs that mature over time. Our conscious mind fills our huge subconscious mind and develops and shapes our conscience. But faith is not facts and figures — it's a feeling based on our knowledge and experiences and what we believe in and what we don't. We are all people of faith.

> Faith is like radar that sees through the fog.
> — Corre Ten Boom

> Reason is our soul's left hand, faith her right.
> — John Donne

It's critical to have faith in the right things. In the thirteenth century theologian Thomas Aquinas added faith, hope and charity to complete what became known as the seven cardinal virtues. Christian apologist J. I. Packer said that faith is the "eye of the soul." So in a sense, we "see" with our faith. We understand through it and act on it. Faith is not blind. If you are feeling at some point that it is, open your "eyes" and seek and acquire more related knowledge and understanding. So faith may be a leap, but a learned one.

The Learner's faith is critical Emotional Avenue in supporting all the Performance Avenues in making them sharper and more practical. Especially for spurring on Innovators, who the more they know, the more they are able intensely and successfully to innovate. See our "Company Network" diagram on our website.

Fairness

From wisdom and faith flows fairness. Fairness is a derivative of justice, another of the seven cardinal virtues. The Learner in us learns what it is to be fair and how to be fair. It's a balance of perception and goodwill. The ever articulate thinker C. S. Lewis offers:

> Justice means much more than the sort of thing that goes on in law courts. It is the old name for everything we should call "fairness"; it includes honesty, give and take, truthfulness, keeping promises, and all that side of life.

In the workplace, a culture of fairness or unfairness is felt by everybody. Industrial-organizational psychologist Deborah Rupp's research reveals:

> How employees perceive a workplace and react to that perception can profoundly affect their physical and emotional health, and in turn, affect an organization's bottom line. A sense of justice may build commitment, loyalty, and a sense of well-being at work, whereas a sense of injustice may spark hostility, aggression, counterproductive behaviors, absenteeism, and even quitting one's job..... Employees seem to have a universal concern for fairness that transcends the self. This leads workers to expect their employer to not only treat its workforce fairly, but to also be a responsible social citizen. Our research, and that of others, has shown that individuals who perceive an organization as being socially responsible are more likely to

seek employment from that firm, less likely to quit, and more likely to engage in positive citizenship behaviors themselves at work.

David Rock in *Your Brain at Work* backs this up and emphasizes how intrinsically rewarding a culture of fairness can be for individuals and companies. He adds the concepts of relatedness, safety, and trust to the mix:

> The feeling you get from a sense of fairness is one of connecting safely with others, so it's linked to relatedness. When you feel someone is being fair, there is also a feeling of increased trust.

As we all know, exercising fairness is easier said than done. Fairness takes a conscious effort that goes from thinking to feeling. We need to first clear our brains of mindsets, preconceptions, biases and prejudices. We need to ask ourselves if we are being fair. We have to point out appropriately and specifically to others that they are not being fair to us. The Golden Rule for us is to treat others fairly and to ask them to treat us fairly. Fairness just doesn't happen, though it can become more of a habit the more we practice it.

You can just feel it

When Learners are in touch with their emotions of curiosity, patience, wisdom, faith and fairness and other relevant and actionable emotions, they are better Learners. Do you as a Learner: have the curiosity to inquire, the patience to observe carefully, the wisdom to make seasoned decisions, the faith that nurtures confidence in yourself, and the fairness that creates a culture of loyalty and trust? Can you really feel it?

Emotional Avenues of the Innovator

Emotional Avenues of the Innovator

We have lots of emotions on all five of our avenues, but it strikes me that the Innovator in us is the most emotional. Somehow when we are on a track to discover something new and different, our juices are flowing the fastest and we are the most excited. That's why we can be so elated when we hit on something that has an impact on our organization or conversely, disappointed when one of our great ideas is not accepted. There are a lot of ups and downs with the creative process.

What's an Innovator? Kirton's Adaption-Innovation Inventory (KAI) formulated by renowned British psychologist Dr. Michael Kirton defines an Innovator this way:

1. Is ingenious, original, independent and unconventional.
2. Challenges problem definition.
3. Does things differently.
4. Discovers problems and avenues for their solutions.
5. Manipulates problems by questioning existing assumptions.
6. Acts as catalyst to unsettled groups and is irreverent of their consensual views.
7. Can perform routine work (system maintenance) for only short bursts.
8. Quickly delegates routine tasks.

9. Tends to take control in unstructured situations.
10. Is seen as unsound, impractical, abrasive, undisciplined, insensitive, and as one who loves to create confusion.
From: *Chemical.Innovation, November 2001, Vol. 31, No. 11, pp 14-22.*

Our research has maintained from the beginning that one's Performance Type is built into their DNA, but that by awareness and training one can enhance their abilities to be a better Leader, Learner, Innovator, Manager or Promoter. The Innovator's DNA project found at http://innovatorsdna.com/about/ confirms this concept for the Innovator, with the realization that Managers are on their own distinct avenue, by the study summarized here:

> The Innovator's DNA emerged from an eight-year collaborative study that sought to uncover the origins of innovative—and often disruptive— business ideas. We interviewed nearly a hundred inventors of revolutionary products and services, as well as founders and CEOs of game-changing companies built on innovative business ideas. Our goal was to understand as much about these people as possible, including the moment (when and how) they came up with the creative ideas that ultimately evolved into new products, services, or businesses. As we reflected on the interviews, we identified five discovery skills that distinguish innovative entrepreneurs and executives from execution focused, results driven managers:
>
> - *Questioning*: Asking questions that challenge common wisdom
> - *Observing*: Scrutinizing customer, supplier, and competitor behaviors to identify new ways of doing things
> - *Networking*: Meeting people with different ideas, backgrounds, and perspectives

- *Experimenting*: Constructing interactive experiences that provoke unorthodox responses to see what insights emerge
- *Associating*: Connecting the unconnected across questions, problems, or ideas from unrelated fields

We can increase our creative intelligence by practicing these five discovery skills. If we challenge the status quo, observe behaviors carefully, dialog with different kinds of people, experiment with the unorthodox, and connect various seemingly unrelated dots, we can boost our creativity and our innovation, which I refer to as "applied creativity."

The Emotional Avenues that are most closely associated with the Innovator and the Innovator in us are daring, perseverance, vulnerability, independence and optimism. Let's start with the Innovator's hardest driving feeling at work, daring.

Daring

Daring is the prime emotion underlying and motivating the Innovator. Daring is a close cousin of courage, the leading emotion of the Leader. Daring is different since it involves a much higher degree of risk and exposure. The Innovator is always out there daring to come up with new ideas and tying his or her best to communicate them and see if they work. It's leaving your comfort zone, constantly risking failure, and sorting through and overcoming all kinds of obstacles.

In my youth my friends and I dared each other to do mostly risky, even stupid things. We didn't want to called a "chicken," so we went ahead and did the dare. On one occasion, about a dozen of my youthful friends and I swam across a river during a raging flood which was the dumbest thing I ever did. But I'm not talking here about the daring feeling at work in this light — daring people need not be fools at all. But rather bold and adventuresome and willing to stick their necks out with calculated risk, not chance. Innovators often have a very high Return on Investment (ROI) on the investment of their time and resources. Venture capital that backs inventors also seeks that kind of ROI. Futurist Alvin Toffler said that, "'It is better to err on the side of daring than the side of caution." And writer and photographer Sir Cecil Beaton asserts:

> Be daring, be different, be impractical, be anything that will assert integrity of purpose and imaginative vision against the play-it-safers, the creatures of the commonplace, the slaves of the ordinary.

Dig deep if you haven't already. Dare to be daring and feel the difference and excitement of trying something new — or better yet, creating something new.

Perseverance

Perseverance is a corollary of daring. We can be daring for a season, but often give up when obstacles mount or when our ideas are opposed by others. Daring folks have a vision and stick with it to its logical, appropriate, and full conclusion. They go beyond the usual, expected or normal — they are persistent, they are perseverant. To keep going, a relook at our self-image may be required. We need to realize that what people think about us may be much less important than tapping into our creative side and pursuing our next innovation. Inventor Thomas Edison asserted, "Many of life's failures are people who did not realize how close they were to success when they gave up." Edison was truly a resilient man — one who always came back from dead-end experiments that others would consider a failure, but to him was only one more approach to solving a problem that didn't pan out. He had little emotion for what people thought of his methodology or crankiness.

In a similar vein, psychologist B. F. Skinner counseled, "A failure is not always a mistake. It may simply be the best one can do under the circumstances. The real mistake is to stop trying." In 2Peter 1: 5-7, the Bible integrates perseverance with virtue, knowledge, self-control, godliness, kindness and love — and that's pretty good company.

Since following the easy path is more comfortable, feeling perseverant can be a real challenge at times. It calls for developing a deep belief in what you are working on and the ultimate purpose it will serve. Soldier, soldier on.

Vulnerability

OK — listen up — this is a hugely important topic! Dr. Brené Brown's 2010 TEDxHouston Talk has had nearly 19 million views. What in the world is she saying? To her, vulnerability is "the origin point for innovation, adaptability, accountability, and visionary leadership." Far from being a weakness, she has found through 12 years of research that vulnerability is a strength, especially one of courage and truthfulness. In her book, the "Power of Vulnerability," she asserts:

> In our culture, we associate vulnerability with emotions we want to avoid such as fear, shame, and uncertainty. Yet we too often lose sight of the fact that vulnerability is also the birthplace of joy, belonging, creativity, authenticity, and love.

Vulnerability is simply being open and honest about who we really are, what we actually know, and what we are transparently doing. It's a very healthy emotion that often takes a lot of concerted effort to fully feel. In her book "Daring Greatly," Brown quotes Peter Sheahan (page 65, hardcover), a consultant on behavioral change to clients such as Apple and IBM:

If you want a culture of creativity and innovation, where sensible risks are embraced on both a market and individual level, start by developing the ability of managers to cultivate an openness to vulnerability in their teams. And this, paradoxically perhaps, requires first that they are vulnerable themselves. This notion that the leader needs to be "in charge" and to "know all the answers" is both dated and destructive. Its impact on others is the sense that they know less, and that they are less than. A recipe for risk aversion if I ever have heard it. Shame becomes fear. Fear leads to risk aversion. Risk aversion kills innovation.

Starting to feel a little more vulnerable? Once we feel daring and perseverant, we can open up to vulnerability and cast aside our shame and fear in the emotional process of allowing our and our organization's innovative spirit to flourish. In my long business career this was an area of success for me. At staff meetings in my building company, I encouraged everyone to lay it all out and fully interact with each other in order to come to sound team decisions. What do you think? How do you feel about this? These were the important questions. This atmosphere allowed us to brainstorm together without anyone being put down. I made it clear that no idea was a bad idea. Our company thrived through innovation that for many years allowed us to stay on the cutting edge in the design and construction of 500 new homes.

Independence

For the Innovator in us to be successful, he or she needs to be dependent on and immersed in an organizational culture that that has a clear effective process of allowing innovation itself to have its maximum positive impact. Too often there's a culture of inertia that is hard to move — there is more "we cannot do this" than "we can do this." There is too much time spent on defining problems than in creating alternative "what if" solutions. An organization thrives on a sustainable basis when and only when there is a welcoming free flow of ideas at all levels.

I have been in a number of situations on non-profit boards where I pushed for more transparency and exchange of strategic thoughts and feelings — all towards opening the innovation window as wide as possible. Organizations need to spend more time discussing what they will be doing to be more successful in three or five years into the future than they are now. And they need to champion Innovators as well as recognize their "early adopter" friends whose loyal support is often critical to the success of their new ideas. Great Innovators are often introverts — but they need to attend meetings and keep up to date on everything in order to be most creative with the tasks at hand. The more they know, they more they can innovate.

But that is where dependence stops and independence begins. Within that framework, the Innovator needs to have a sense of independence — *strong inner feelings of freedom, autonomy and self-reliance with a measured appropriate pushback against control, influence and authority.* The Innovator needs to be unique and distinct, create their own space to work and play in, and be ready, willing and able to stand on their own. Their *default* position must be to *detach*. They have to be comfortable feeling their independence while at the same time contributing to the mission and vision of the organization.

Sometimes the "herd" makes a good decision. Take buffaloes of the old wild west for example. They would normally come to a consensus about where to graze next. But when Native Americans stealthily herded them into a stampede over a buffalo jump (a very steep slope in the middle of an open prairie) in order for the buffaloes to break their necks, it would have been better to separate from the herd. You won't get your neck broken by being a constant follower at work, nor will you separate from the herd with a new great idea. But be an independent thinker-feeler and notice what comes to you that might make a difference.

Optimism

Optimism is simply the hope that the future can and will be as bright as possible. As I mentioned in the section on faith, hope is one the seven cardinal virtues that was added to the first four from the biblical call to have faith, hope and charity. The Innovator has a positive attitude and is confident in the future. There does need to be a balance — optimism must be tied to realism. Optimism looks at what are reasonable stretch goals. Both the "reasonable" and the "stretch" parts are critical. We can hope too little or too much.

But there also needs to be much more of an emphasis on *how we can do something* — solutions, than on *why we cannot do something* — problems. As president of my company and as a non-profit board chair, I too often heard about not being able to do something — sometimes even before we looked proactively and closely at how we might be able to do it.

The Innovator in us needs to feel his or her optimism. They look for opportunities in all circumstances and are careful not to define "impossible" too narrowly. They follow the Navy Seabees motto "Can do!" Think and feel like Walt Disney, Martin Luther King, Jr. and Ronald Reagan.

You can just feel it

When Innovators are in touch with their emotions of daring, perseverance, vulnerability, independence and optimism and other relevant and actionable emotions, they are better Innovators. Do you as an Innovator: fearlessly push the envelope, stick with your projects, strive to be open and honest, focus on being unique and distinct, and have realistic optimism? Can you really feel it?

Emotional Avenues of the Manager

The Emotional Avenues of the Manager

In the last section we indicated that Innovators are the most openly emotional. Managers, on the other hand, are the ones who need to be aware of and control their emotions the most. Not that Managers do not make decisions with their emotions, but theirs is the realm of direction, discipline and steadiness. They are the steely-eyed sensates that drive toward outcomes in a calm organized way. Managers wear emotions, but not on their sleeves.

So the five emotional avenues of the Manager and the Manager in us — authenticity, pride, commitment, sensing and empathy — are well grounded and proven emotions that support the process of here is what we need to do, so let's go and do it. It's planning and efficiency that takes emotions to the edge of their matter-of-factness. Managers are the ones who tend to think that thinking is everything and that feeling gets in the way. But the more they leverage their thoughts AND their feelings and those of their sphere of influence, they better they manage.

So how does the Manager get from Point A of interpreting the strategy to Point B of executing the mission with effective and efficient use of their positive emotions? By being real, taking pride in their work, being totally committed, being sensitive and observant, and caring about what their people are feeling. Combine that with their logical step-by-step thinking and the job gets done and done well.

Authenticity

Everyone in the workplace needs to be authentic, but none more than Managers. Why do I say this? Because when you are dealing with organization, production and outcomes, there is an especially high expectation that you be really real, to the point, and on target. The time for politicking, avoidance and appeasement is long past — the rubber is hitting the road, period.

The emotion of authenticity is a huge topic in today's modern business world. The articles on the subject often start out with a caveat about not being overly transparent about information, particularly personal information, that is — not relevant and actionable to the subject or task at hand. Fair enough, I agree. There may not be a need to say everything you think and feel — your role may not require that much transparency. Yes, we want to lay it all out, but need to limit our conversations to what bears on the matters at hand — they can't therefore be too much about us and must be focused on what moves the ball forward.

Most effective authenticity for the Manager, and the Manager in us, is simply being honest, open and complete. And that can mean cutting through our tendency to live in denial about matters we don't want to discuss or even, undenounced to us, we have misguided views on. Honesty sometimes takes soul-searching work, openness can be uncomfortable, and completeness is too easy to avoid. And yet interaction between direct reports and a Manager or between team members will not be successful without all three.

Pride

Pride is a master emotion that, on its dark side, underlies a lot of other emotions and behavior. Biblically speaking, pride comes before destruction which comes before a fall since it is focused on the self and is independent of God. Pride leads to self-righteousness, hubris and arrogance. This is not the kind of pride we are dealing with in this section, but is mentioned for reference and context. Pride has many definitions — we will be looking briefly at the healthy kind that is important to the Manager.

There's a wholesome sense of pride when we say, "I'm proud of her work" or "I'm proud of you, son." The Manager in us is responsible for the quality of a product or service and for satisfactory outcomes of everything under his or her oversight. So it's critical to have a good self-image and be proud of what we do in the workplace. "Taking pride in our work" is an age-old adage that is as true today as it always has been.

And people are constantly observing the Manager — if he or she wants to do it well, then we need to do the same thing. Pride in what we do or make is directly reflected in the success of any organization. It's an emotional buy-in to an approach that ultimately affects vendors, customers, shareholders, and all other stakeholders. *Healthy pride breeds excellence.*

Commitment

The Manager in us knows full well that without being dedicated to the task at hand, it will not get done well. While the Leader has passion for the mission and vision, the Manager has commitment to execution by focusing on objectives. Commitment is felt loyalty, earnestness and sincerity. It's a duty and all-out engagement and involvement in the cause.

Commitment is one of those things that a lot more easily said than done. It can take time for it to become an emotional habit that turns into a course of action. Commitment keeps us track especially when distractions and other objectives get in the way. Look around and see successful people and you will see long-term commitment to whatever they are doing.

But what makes us commit to something? One motivation I have found is reflecting on our purpose in life. The *Purpose Driven Life* by Pastor Rick Warren, which has been read by untold millions around the world and deserves to be read and reread, puts the true meaning of life and our place in it in clear understanding and rich perspective. It's a game changer. I leave it to you reader to go through its 40 insightful chapters and come to your own conclusions. The main point is that as we develop purpose and meaning in life, we also develop commitment to a positive tailor-made vison and mission for our lives that includes our work and careers.

Sensing

The Manager in us has an emotional sense about things — call it unconscious feeling. Something feels right or it doesn't with levels uncertainty in between. Intuition is more about unconscious thinking, or well, instinctively knowing about something. The Myers-Briggs Type Indicator (MBTI) can be a good indicator of the amounts of our natural gifts of sensing and intuition. My wife Gayle is a deeply sensing person and it's been my experience that women are generally better at sensing than men. She can read people and their motives very well. Shakespeare was a master sensate in the way he, for example, curiously but deftly felt and exposed the evil plots of the cunning characters in his plays.

Improving our sensing ability is like improving our emotional intelligence. Daniel Goleman and many other researchers and authors have proposed ways to do this which can be easily accessed. Closely observe how good sensates are able to size up people and events and get the right answers about people's emotional intent. The old standbys such as understanding body language and responding to changes in someone's tone of voice are always helpful.

If a Manager is saying that he or she has trouble understanding why people act as they do or why events unfold as they do, perhaps they need to look for another position that is less Manager oriented. A Manager needs to have a fearless emotional sense of how to react, what needs to be done, and who is best at doing it.

Empathy

Everybody needs to have empathy at work, but none more than the Manager who has to work well with others to get things done. Empathy is very challenging and often overlooked as a critically important emotion. As Theodore Roosevelt stated, "Nobody cares how much you know, until they know how much you care."

I like the twelve-point summary of empathy in the work environment by Tranveer Nasser, leadership coach, speaker and writer:

- Empathy allows us to feel safe with our failures because we won't simply be blamed for them.
- It encourages leaders to understand the root cause behind poor performance.
- Being empathetic allows leaders to help struggling employees improve and excel.
- Empathy allows leaders to build and develop relationships with those they lead.
- Demonstrating empathy is hard; it's takes time and effort to demonstrate awareness and understanding.
- It's not always easy to understand why an employee thinks or feels the way they do about a situation.

- It means putting others ahead of yourself which can be a challenge in today's competitive workplace.
- Many organizations are focused on achieving goals no matter what the cost to employees.
- You gain a greater awareness of the needs of your employees.
- Empathy allows you to create an environment of open communication and more effective feedback.
- It allows us to understand and explore problems employees face and how to help them resolve them.
- Being empathetic with your employees helps to validate what they're going through.
(http://www.tanveernaseer.com/why-empathy-matters-in-leadership/)

Put yourself in the other person's shoes. Feel how they feel and approach them accordingly. Feel their pain and struggles and feel their joy and successes too.

You can just feel it

When Managers are in touch with their emotions of authenticity, pride, commitment, sensing and empathy, other relevant and actionable emotions, they are better Managers. Do you as a Manager: have the authenticity to be realistic, the pride to maintain quality, the commitment to carrying out the mission, the sensing to read people, and the empathy to show you care and understand? Can you really feel it?

Emotional Avenues of the Promoter

The Emotional Avenues of the Promoter

For the Promoter, and the Promoter in us, emotions play the most significant role in driving our behavior and thereby need the most attention and polishing. And more so than the other avenues, if the Promoter is having a bad day, he or she especially needs to "fake it until they make it." The Promoter who is primarily a communicator cannot afford poor communication by allowing negative feelings to surface to a blatant or obvious level.

The five emotions of the Promoter — appeal (attraction), engagement (involvement), encouragement (support), appreciation (thankfulness) and amusement (fun) — are deeply felt as well as "worn on our sleeve." And that's a good thing that is critical to the success of an individual, a team, or a company. All the other avenues are less effective without the understanding personal touch that provides for people to like us and our brand.

Want to be perceived, present, and persuade well? First, create an emotional bond and buy-in with your audience. The more the "appeal" of the messenger, the more the message is seen in a positive light. Just ask any politician — and remember, like it or not, in one way or another, we are all politicians.

Appeal

"Appeal" is the number one emotional draw to the Promoter and the Promoter in us because it's deeper and more encompassing then "attractive." Parallels would be joy versus happiness and prudence versus wisdom. Being appealing includes a whole bundle of adjectives such as attractive, inviting, charming, desirable, endearing, alluring, and winsome.

We have demonstrated that emotions are a big factor in decision-making — it's not only how we feel about something, but how we feel about the person or persons communicating those emotions. So it can be a negative, or hopefully a positive, double whammy — that is, the content of the both message and the messenger. Being appealing can make all the difference in communicating bad news — or good news — in a way that is as well received by the listener as possible.

Are you appealing? Do people want to be around you even if they disagree with you? Try this. Think and feel about someone at work that you agree with but don't like. Is it because they need to work on being more appealing as in maybe ingratiating and considerate? Too often we don't fully realize that being liked, at the least not being disliked, is critical to promoting ourselves and our ideas. So maximize your charm and do all you can to be winsome.

Engagement

Psychological engagement at work is critical for the Promoter since it bonds the communicator and the listener. It is such a strong emotion, that we get "engaged" to be married. But engagement may take extra work since it's not always a natural comfortable emotion. For example, some like me have an avoidant attachment style and have to be more deliberate in our attention to others and their feelings.

In engaging someone, we want to directly relate to and connect with them. We need to be "all-in" and "two-way" including eye contact and body language. We need to pay attention to, listen to, interpret, and understand others. This engagement, especially a culture of it, leads to job involvement, improvement and satisfaction, commitment to the organization, and motivation. It's impossible to be inspired and passionate or seek to meet goals and maintain the highest values without engaging and being engaged.

And in order to be engaged with people at work, we similarly need to be engaged with the actual work itself which is measured by vigor, dedication and absorption:

> Work engagement is most often defined as a positive, fulfilling, work-related state of mind that is characterized by vigor, dedication, and absorption. In essence, work engagement captures how workers experience their work: as stimulating and energetic and something to which they really want to devote time and effort (the vigor component); as a significant and meaningful pursuit (dedication); and as engrossing and something on which they are fully concentrated (absorption).
> (http://www.arnoldbakker.com/workengagement.php)

Encouragement

Encouragement is an important way that the Promoter expresses and acts on their engagement. Once engaged we enhance that engagement by encouraging others. They can feel it and it feels great! Encouragement can create a strong emotional bond. It advocates, supports, inspires, gives hope — and well, promotes. It motivates people to do their best.

And perhaps most importantly encouragement helps get you through the tough times. When we are down, we can always use a coworker to lift us up.

> *Don't let the muggles get you down.*
> J.K. Rowling, *Harry Potter and the Prisoner of Azkaban*

Sincere and genuine encouragement is something that sticks with you and keeps you going. It's positive reinforcement of the good that is in us and puts obstacles in our path in the right perspective. It helps us move on and face change with confidence. Encouragement builds us up in ways we cannot do by ourselves. Put your arm around someone and say, "Good job!" They will respond to it and remember it for a long time.

Appreciation

Appreciation is a powerful and effective emotion. A Promoter's engagement leads to encouragement and then to appreciation — three vital parts of the connective tissue needed to be winsome and persuasive. Appreciation is critical to any good relationship and the more we think it, feel it, and act it, the more the relationship thrives. We can always find something to thank someone for, but sometimes we don't do it enough.

> *Thank you, thank you very much!*
> Elvis Presley

I'm a big Elvis fan and enjoyed visiting his Graceland homestead in Memphis. He was a great entertainer and the consummate Promoter. And he always took the time to genuinely thank his audience several times. He meant it and they felt it.

Thanking someone makes you more appealing, is an act of sharing and humility, and levels the playing field of communication. When showing appreciation, the Promoter in us is acknowledging that the other person is important and well worth relating to. Done right then, active appreciation is a bonding experience between presenter and listener that enhances the presentation and perks up the listener.

Amusement

I'm such a strong believer in the need and effectiveness of positive humor in every aspect of life, especially in often tense workplace, that I authored a collection of poems entitled "Finding Your Clown." I like this quote for Wikipedia (https://en.wikipedia.org/wiki/Office_humor):

> Humor is an inevitable part of the social environment of work, and has been argued to be a potential tool for improving worker satisfaction and organizational results. Studies have suggested that humor can increase worker cohesiveness, creativity, motivation, and resilience in the face of adversity.

For *Emotional Avenues* we apply the emotions associated with amusement as a broader concept that includes entertainment and recreation. We all need to humble ourselves at times and not take ourselves quite so seriously. The lighter side of things gives us the balance we need to perform best at work.

Above all Promoters need to perfect their social skills and that includes a strong dose of humor and entertainment and the social interactive opportunities provided by recreational activities. Fun, smiles, hugs and laughter are tools that make us much more successful in all our endeavors.

You Can Just Feel It

When Promoters are in touch with their emotions of appeal, engagement, encouragement, appreciation and amusement, other relevant and actionable emotions, they are better Promoters. Do you as a Promoter: have the appeal to be attractive, the engagement to connect well, the encouragement to support and inspire, the appreciation to relate with sharing and humility, and the amusement to provide fun and balance? Can you really feel it?

Some Final Feelings

Some Final Feelings

Loving One Another at Work

Lovie one another at work. What? Isn't that getting a little gushy and weird? *Actually love is the umbrella over all the 25 emotions we have discussed in this book! Love is the master positive emotion* (and fear is the master negative emotion). If we don't talk about emotions enough in the workplace, we certainly aren't going to talk about loving one another there either. And that's a pretty big problem these days. We either don't know how to love one another at work or we are not motivated to do so. And yet the foremost commandment in both the Old and New Testaments after loving God is to love one another. What does that mean? While we don't have room here to go deeply into this subject except to point out how important it is, here is a sampling of what biblical love in action:

> 4 Love is patient, love is kind. It does not envy, it does not boast, it is not proud. 5 It does not dishonor others, it is not self-seeking, it is not easily angered, it keeps no record of wrongs. 6 Love does not delight in evil but rejoices with the truth. 7 It always protects, always trusts, always hopes, always perseveres. 8a Love never fails.
>
> 1 Corinthians 13 (NIV)

Our relationships with others and our work environment might be vastly different if we had loving one another as a first principle. We would, for example, put others before ourselves and think and feel love before we acted. No, it would not solve all our problems at work (it might even create some), but it would be the best framework for us to succeed as individuals, teams and companies. Transcendence will always trump the here and now. Our loving attitude, including tough love, towards others is more important than winning, though both can be achieved.

Our Gut Feelings

For the past 20 years neuroscientists have been studying the nervous system circuits in our bodies' abdominal area and have discovered that these circuits, which are connected to our brains through our spine, have a profound effect on our decision making. They often refer to these circuits as our "second brain." Here's an interesting description of business management outcomes resulting from this phenomenon:

> Economist Shabnam Mousavi of the Johns Hopkins Carey Business School conducts research in an area known as "fast and frugal heuristics." Heuristics are the mental shortcuts that we develop to lessen the cognitive burden of decision making. In certain scenarios, that fast-thinking intuition is better than rational and deliberate calculation. Mousavi was lead author of an article on this topic in March 2014 in the Journal of Business Research. Business leaders claim that they use objective methods when making decisions. *But on closer inspection, it has been found that executives admit to relying on "gut feel" quite regularly.* Rather than minimizing the value of such decision making, Mousavi says, we should recognize the evolutionary reasons humans developed these approaches and figure out when it's best to use them.*Johns Hopkins Health Review, Volume 2, Issue 1*

So paying attention to our gut in terms of its interconnected physical, mental and emotional health is critical to our wellbeing and to how successful we are at making decisions. When you gut tells you something, listen carefully and decipher and apply its instant message as best and as fast as you can.

Reelin' Feelin'

One well emphasized element of depression is commonly referred to as *stinkin' thinkin'* — that is, dwelling on bad thoughts and imagining bad things at the expense of good thoughts and imaginings. Similarly what I call *reelin' feelin'* is dwelling on negative feelings like anger, control and sadness that crowd out feelings of thankfulness, confidence and joy. We reel backwards rather than move forward.

Ever have a *reelin' feelin'* or two? What is it based on? Does recognizing it and naming it help? It's complicated and we're not going to resolve it here, but be aware that unsubstantiated and unnecessary bad felling, just like bad thinking, can get us down and keep us there. Look out, look up, and let faith and balance set you free.

The Five Senses

Our avenues are interconnected and work together like our five senses. Some of our senses are better than others. For example, I'm very nearsighted but have excellent hearing. So we can be stronger with one sense or one avenue and weaker on another, but we can perform well if all the senses, as with all avenues, compensate for and complement one other. A curious application of both Performance Avenues and Emotional Avenues breaks down this way:

    Vision — Leader
    Hearing — Learner

Smell — Innovator
Taste — Manager
Touch — Promoter

Emotional Avenues and Performance Types

Author and executive coach Marshall Goldsmith's research presented in his book "Triggers" indicates that we are not very good at assessing *how well* we perform at work and tend to strongly overrate it. From my 13 years of talent development experience, I believe the same can be true for determining *how* we perform. So we need intuitive and applicable tools to get the best answer. On our website at www.PerformanceAvenues.com under the *Self-Assessment* tab, we address Emotional Avenues as another way of helping you determine your primary Performance Avenue, which will subsequently lead you to determine your Performance Type (see our *Advanced* tab):

> Assessments and descriptions of work traits and types have traditionally centered much more on thinking than feeling. And yet feeling drives our reasoning and behavior more or less as much as thinking and more so in quick decision-making. So we need to think and feel about our emotions in order to get the right handle on our reasoning and behavior at work and in the rest of our lives. We can't just think though a problem, we have to feel through it as well. For example, the Manager, above all else, needs to be firmly in touch with reality — and his or her level of "authenticity." The Promoter needs to understand his or her level of how well they "appeal" to others. Each Performance Avenue below has five "Emotional Avenues" that underlie and relate to it. See how well these emotions align with you. Be aware of your emotions at work and how they drive your behavior and decision-making.

So it's not just how we perform at work, but also how we feel as we are go about our job. With a Performance Type of Learner-Innovator, I am primarily daring and optimistic, but also curious and seek to be wise. How about you?

Performance Avenues and Emotional Avenues, though not formal assessments using questionnaires, are *guides that can be considered when hiring or promoting someone*. First, do not get too emotional about these important decisions — that is, use the right amount of gut feeling when hiring or promoting. Secondly, when hiring or promoting someone, look at emotions for their respective jobs. For example, if a Leader position, look specifically at their courage, trust and inspiration.

Feeling How We Work

As the subtitle of this book indicates, we not only want you to know how you work as in which Performance Avenues, but how you *feel* at work on those avenues. For example, we can't just know that we are an Innovator or know about the Innovator in us, we need to feel and experience our perseverance and vulnerability. As a Leader, we need to feel and experience our courage and trust. And as a Promoter, we need to feel and experience our engagement and encouragement, and so on with all five avenues and all 25 emotions. It takes a little time and practice, but eventually it becomes intuitively second nature. AND we begin to feel more and have a higher sensitivity to our emotions and how they are connected to our behavior and decision making at work.

Journal of Catching Yourself Feeling at Work

To me a journal is simply writing about our individual journeys through a part of our lives or about a subject that affects our lives including the all-important "aha" moments worth an entry in our journal. Ken Blanchard made popular the notion of catching someone doing something right. Apply that to the positive emotions we has discussed in this book, when we find ourselves say being especially passionate, vulnerable or amusing, make note of it on the corresponding page of this journal under Passion, Vulnerability or Amusement. Try to make an entry on all 25 emotions in the first 25 days of beginning this journal. *This exercise will also see more clearly which Emotional Avenues and subsequently which Performance Avenues you travel on most naturally, comfortably and effectively.*

You hear it all the time, but there are rewards for writing something down that includes focusing our attention, reinforcing its value, and allowing us to make it part of us going forward. There's a page in this journal for each of the following emotions:

Courage

Trust

Inspiration

Passion

Humility

Curiosity

Patience

Wisdom

Faith

Fairness

Daring

Perseverance

Vulnerability

Independence

Optimism

Authenticity

Pride

Commitment

Sensing

Empathy

Appeal

Engagement

Encouragement

Appreciation

Amusement

COURAGE

TRUST

INSPIRATION

PASSION

HUMILITY

CURIOSITY

PATIENCE

WISDOM

FAITH

FAIRNESS

DARING

PERSEVERANCE

VULNERABILITY

INDEPENDENCE

OPTIMISM

AUTHENTICITY

PRIDE

COMMITMENT

SENSING

EMPATHY

Journal of Catching Yourself Feeling at Work

APPEAL

ENGAGEMENT

ENCOURAGEMENT

APPRECIATION

AMUSEMENT

www.ingramcontent.com/pod-product-compliance
Lightning Source LLC
LaVergne TN
LVHW051957060526
838201LV00059B/3694